SILVER MEDAL WINNER

PRESIDENT'S BOOK AWARD

FLORIDA AUTHORS AND
PUBLISHERS ASSOCIATION

2022

To Charlotte ~
Your special light
blesses all on the path
with you.

Keep on shining!

Rising together...
Ann Marie
Acacio

RISE AND SHINE

RECLAIMING OUR
RIGHTFUL PLACE

Ann Marie Acacio

Typography & Production by Hallard Press LLC/John W Prince

Published by Hallard Press LLC.
www.HallardPress.com   Info@HallardPress.com   352-234-6099
Bulk copies of this book can be ordered at Info@HallardPress.com

Printed in the United States of America   1

Publisher's Cataloging-in-Publication data

Names: Acacio, Ann Marie, author.
Title: Rise and shine : reclaiming our rightful place / Ann Marie Acacio.
Description: The Villages, FL: Hallard Press, 2021.
Identifiers: LCCN: 2021912158 | ISBN: 978-1-951188-29-0 (paperback) | 978-1-951188-30-6 (ebook)
Subjects: LCSH Self-actualization (Psychology)--Religious aspects--Christianity. | Christian living. | Conduct of life. | Christianity and other religions--New Age movement. | BISAC BODY, MIND & SPIRIT / Inspiration & Personal Growth | BODY, MIND & SPIRIT / Spiritualism | RELIGION / Christian Living / Personal Growth | SELF-HELP / Personal Growth / General | SELF-HELP / Spiritual
Classification: LCC BV4598.2 .A33 2021 | DDC 158--dc23

ISBN: 978-1-951188-29-0 (Paperback)
ISBN: 978-1-951188-30-6 (Ebook)

What others say about *Rise and Shine*...

"A metaphysics primer! In this book of accessible wisdom, complex concepts are explained simply by author/teacher/minister Ann Marie. What you can comprehend, you can embody."

—*Rev. Linda Martella-Whitsett, VP Unity Prayer Ministry at Unity World Headquarters, author* Divine Audacity

"*RISE AND SHINE* is a call to every spiritual seeker to do the work that is ours to do. Rev. Ann Marie weaves together keen insights lifting us higher in consciousness and stories encouraging us to fulfill our destiny as "lights of the world." Chapter by chapter, revelation by revelation, life story by life story, we are not only called to rise and shine; we are shown the way to a life of practical spirituality."

—*Jim Rosemergy, minister and author* The Watcher, The Third Coming.

DEDICATION

"Grace isn't a little prayer you chant before receiving a meal. It's a way to live."—Jacqueline Winspea

This book is dedicated, with much appreciation, first, to my wonderfully-supportive husband, Bob, who never gave up on us, despite all my long hours of study and ministering.

It is, also, dedicated to our loving and extra-special children, Bob, Jr., Janine and Suzanne. I am SO thankful for your understanding as I endeavored to wear the many hats of daughter, wife, mom, grandma, nana, student, teacher. minister, chaplain, author, friend, etc., not necessarily in that order.

I also, dedicate it to my Mom and Dad, Ann and Steve Zumchak (both of blessed memory) who, even though they were skeptical and critical of my studies at first, did an about-face and supported my journey of spiritual rediscovery. Thanks, Mom, for all the newsletters and Sunday bulletins you folded, draperies you sewed for the Sanctuary, pierogies and pot pies you helped package for our fundraisers, and especially for the times you played the devil's advocate. I learned so much through it all.

TABLE OF CONTENTS

Dedication v

Preface ix

Introduction.. xv

Part One: How the Mind Works

  1: What I Believe 3

  2: How Consciousness Works 9

    The Hundredth Monkey 11

  3: Conscious / Sub-Conscious Areas of Mind 13

    The Drama Begins 17

    And Then There was... 19

  4: A Look at the Soul 23

    Reinforcing the Concept 24

  5: A New Look at Evil 29

    Is there a devil? 30

    The Law of Mind Action 31

    Going Beyond the Law of Mind Action 33

  6: The Super Conscous Area of Mind 37

    A Lesson from Brother Lawrence 38

    Tuning to Concert Pitch 39

    Going Beyond Concert Pitch 40

    More Than Enough 41

    Let There Be Light 42

    Small "t" or Capital "T" 43

  7: Moving Into Action 45

    What is New Thought Christianity? 46

From Reel to Real 48

Opening the Door 48

No Fault Assurance 50

Stop Waiting For Forgiveness 51

A Trip to McDonald's 52

It Takes Practice 53

Expansion and Contraction 53

Part 2: The Trinity

8: What is the Trinity? 57

The Human Trinity 59

The Trinity in Traditional Christianity 60

The Hebrew Trinity 63

9: Understanding the Metaphysical Trinity 67

Turning Our Focus Upside Down 69

Energy Continually Moves 70

Pay Attention to the Feedback 71

Filling the Vacuum 71

The Final Piece of the Puzzle 74

Reclaiming Our Rightful Place 74

10: Living From our Rightful Place 77

A Lesson From a Children's Fairy Tale 78

Being Called to the Deafening Silence 79

From Peduncle to the Next Phylum 81

11: Practices for Anchoring Our Spiritual Nature ... 89

The Prayer of the Chalice 91

Franciscan Benediction 95

Acknowledgments 101

About the Author 103

PREFACE

"There are two fatal errors that keep great projects from coming to life...
1) not finishing, and 2) not starting."
— The Buddha

I am a visual learner and teacher. It's really true that, as the Chinese say, "a picture is worth a thousand words." I like to share ideas through the use of diagrams and stories and may be one of a few teachers who still uses a flip chart and markers. As a result, this book contains both images and stories. The following is a snippet of my journey.

I was born and raised Catholic, attended parochial school and received the sacraments faithfully. I even helped Sister Seraphia start the first remedial reading clinic when I was in the 8th grade at Sacred Heart School (1953-54.) I listened to and helped slow readers during my recess and lunchtimes. Feeling very drawn to the spiritual life, I had strongly considered entering the convent.

Then, in my junior year in high school, I met Bob Acacio, who would be my one-and-only love for the past 63 years and counting. So the convent life was no longer even a blip on the radar screen. Yet, the spiritual life always remained important to me.

When Bob and I were in our early 30s, his Mom, Ann, offered to gift us with a course of study in Transcendental Meditation. While Bob was eager to take the course, I strongly resisted. I was too busy taking care of our home and three children and was adamant about not wanting to pursue anything that was outside the belief system in which I felt comfortable at that time.

Bob's Mom asked if I would attend the introductory session and, if I didn't like it, she would never ask me to step out of my comfort zone again. I agreed to attend, just to get her to stop asking me to go to classes.

As life would have it, my curiosity was ignited in the introductory session, so I attended the entire week of classes with her and Bob. Now the stage was set for more to come, since this was my opening to another dimension of possibilities. I felt myself begin to come alive inside as I resonated with ideas shared in classes and books. It was like I had already known these ideas on some level, and now they were being reawakened.

After not having picked up a book since graduating Business College in 1960, I became a voracious reader on metaphysical subjects. Metaphysics = Meta means mind in Greek. It relates to ideas forming in our mind before anything is seen in the physical. The studies became easier for me. On some level it was like having an addiction, and I couldn't get enough.

In 1977 my studies led me to connect with a woman who sent us a gift subscription to a little inspirational booklet called Daily Word, published by Unity School. Bob and I were immediately drawn to its positive reflections, and we felt like we finally found a philosophy that nurtured us on many levels. We then learned about a group called Unity that was starting up in the Lehigh Valley, PA area, and in 1978 we began to travel south for workshops and then for Sunday Services. Living in Wilkes-Barre, in the Wyoming Valley, PA area at that time, it was about an hour's drive south to Allentown.

In September 1979 our little group of truth-seekers, who rode with us to Allentown, decided we wanted to have our own group in Wilkes-Barre. As a result, Bob and I opened up our home, and I began to lead a little study group on September 26, 1979, with guidance from the then-minister of Unity of Lehigh Valley, Rev. Yves Lafontant.

The inner call became very strong to begin personal studies toward becoming a Licensed Unity Teacher. In November 1979, I took my first class for credit in the Licensed Unity Teacher Program, and in March 1983, after exceeding my required credits, I graduated from Unity School for Religious Studies. I continued my studies and was licensed as a Unity Teacher in March 1984, teaching Unity classes at Unity of Lehigh Valley from March 1984 to December 1989.

After the second minister in Wilkes-Barre left in October 1987, I was asked by the Steering Committee to serve as Spiritual Leader of Unity of Wyoming Valley. Of course, my answer was a resounding YES. It was another rite of passage for me to bring the ministry to full membership status in the Association of Unity Churches, now called Unity World-Wide Ministries.

In January 1992 I was accepted into the pilot four-year Field Licensing and Ordination Program at Unity Headquarters in Lee Summit, MO. This Program supports Licensed Teachers leading a ministry to work with a mentor and complete the same requirements as ministerial students in the full two-year residency program. It was an arduous four-year program, yet my passion for ministry went beyond the challenge of the program. I was ordained in my home church on May 11, 1996 by my good friend and colleague, the Rev. Jim Rosemergy.

What a joy it has been to serve this ministry until my retirement on December 31, 2006. During this time I also served Unity ministries in the Binghamton, NY area, Harrisburg, PA and Allentown, PA.

I was also blessed to serve for ten years on the Board of Unity World-Wide Ministries - Eastern Region, serving four of those years as president.

Interfaith work has always been very important to me, and I served for 15 years on the Wyoming Valley Interfaith Council, with six of those years as president. This is in addition to continuing to serve for nearly 35 years in prison ministry, which warms my heart.

So...that's me... the perennial student, always wanting to learn more and inspire more. What I'm sharing in this book is a compilation of ideas I've learned, up until now, along with new ideas that have been intuited through me over the years. I am eager to "pay them forward," as they were shared with me.

INTRODUCTION

"Anyone who wants to write a book should do it. It matters not if the book is technically perfect, if anyone has already written a book like it, or how many people read it. Write it because it must be written." — Alan Cohen

This book is the result of an idea that was birthed through me, when teaching a class, over 25 years ago, on the difference between the traditional Christian Trinity and the Metaphysical Trinity. I've presented this material at many workshops and classes over the years and had previously considered compiling it into a book, yet hadn't done it, up until now.

It is at the strong encouragement of the many students who have attended the workshops, and through my own inner guidance, that I have been inspired to document this information. There has been a plethora of books written on how our mind works and how our thoughts create our reality. Why is this book different?

Part One of this book is a primer on how I believe our mind

works and how it affects our life in each moment. This life-experience, or chapter as I prefer to call it, which begins with birth and ends with our return to spirit, otherwise called death, then affects each subsequent chapter in our one on-going life experience.

Part Two focuses on rediscovering our connection with the Trinity... what the Trinity is from a human standpoint, as well as from my interpretation of the Hebrew, Traditional Christian, and New Thought Christian viewpoints. This leads us to remember what our place is in it.

My goal is to enhance the clarity of our understanding which, in turn, can simplify how we choose to show-up in each moment of our ongoing life experience. My hope is your willingness to be a partner on this journey as, together, we lead each other home.

PART ONE

HOW OUR MIND WORKS

CHAPTER ONE

What I Believe

*"It takes courage to grow up
and become who you really are."*
— E.E. Cummings

Through my many years of various studies and inner spiritual work, I now consider myself a non-theist. I do not believe in a God who resides outside of myself, one who has a personality, who judges and either punishes or blesses us. Nor do I believe in a heaven or hell after we leave these physical forms, or earthsuits as I like to call our bodies. I see heaven and hell as states or consciousness we create, depending on our interpretation of an experience.

I do not create a God in the image and likeness of humankind. I believe in a Presence of Absolute Good that permeates all creation. I have no need to name it. I simply see it as All That Is. Well, perhaps I have named it—for myself. This Presence has no gender. It is an All-Pervading Principle that is Unconditional Love. It is the image and likeness in which we have all been created, without exception, whether we believe it and act on it or not.

I have had people say to me, "I need a personal God, a God that comforts me and works in my life, not just one in principle." Me, too! As I looked at the idea of "principle," I remembered that there are "principles" that I couldn't live without, like the principle of music or the principle of mathematics.

When I feel a down-energy... overwhelmed with a long to-do list, stressed, tight inside, I feel comforted by the principle of music. Music is all-accepting. It doesn't withhold any part of itself from a little child who pounds on the piano and creates dissonance. It doesn't say "you can't use me until you learn how to play." Music simply IS and loves unconditionally. The sound of dissonance is the feedback received when the principle is not being used with a more mature understanding.

Being a lover of music, I apply myself to learning to use this principle in my life so I may enjoy a more refined experience, which blesses and enriches my life. Playing my piano daily adds balance to my life.

There is a question I find important to carry in my heart each day. "Just for today, am I willing to do what is mine to do so I may experience this Presence of Unconditional Love consistently? It seems easy to set this intention at the beginning of each day; yet, as the day unfolds, with all its unpredictable happenings and changes, I realize the value of being flexible. Going with the flow, or as I like to say "flowing with what's going," plays a huge part in fulfilling my intention to be the Love I've come here to be.

Following through and putting the intention into motion assures me my life unfolds with the harmony of this Higher Love in each area... relationships, prosperity, wellness, and purpose. Higher Love goes beyond human love. It loves because its nature is to Love, without having a specific reason, or looking for the same quality of Love in return from people in the outer world.

Can this Unconditional Love really be part of our journey? Not just part of it! It's meant to be our entire journey. It's called Entitlement with a capital E. We may have heard this word used more in-line with individuals who believe they're entitled to worldly prosperity, recognition, etc. to the point that they justify taking it by whatever means they can. If they believe, for whatever reason, that life is being unfair, they may self-medicate in ways that continue to support this unloving and unhealthy belief. Individuals may self-medicate with food, sex, drugs, alcohol, binge-watching TV, even work.

I am, you are, *Entitled* to experience this Presence of Absolute Good on a consistent basis. So, why aren't we? Read on, please.

I believe that the ideas I am sharing can open a new pathway to a journey whose destination takes us right back to the beginning, which is our oneness with all Life. In the beginning there was One - One complete idea of all the possibilities that could ever come into existence in physical form.

In thinking about this idea, I wondered... might the "big bang," what the beginning of life on our planet has been called, simply be the opening up into physical expression of the magnificent potential of all these possibilities?

Perhaps we might compare it to the cracking of an egg. If I were to break the shell of a raw egg, I may find one yolk inside. Yet, other eggs may have two or more yolks, all raw, and all having the same potential to be utilized. I, as the holder of that egg, get to decide whether I want my egg to be baked, fried, scrambled, poached, hard or soft boiled, or simply left raw. There may even be other possibilities I just haven't thought of... yet.

These other possibilities remain in potential until my understanding forms a mental picture in my conscious mind. It is then that I can give form to the idea in the physical, if I choose to act on it. How many ideas might we have had that we didn't act on, at the time, which merely stayed as a possibility? Every invention, piece of music, form of artwork, or new design all started as a possibility. They are brought into form because someone acted on the idea.

I share my understanding of how our mind works so we may, more readily, comprehend the meaning and purpose of our journey through time and space. I find it important that these ideas be preserved for future generations of seekers who keep alive the basic question: "how does life work?"

Questions to ponder...

1. Do you feel that your life is flowing? What led you to pick-up this book and engage with the ideas in it?

2. Have you noticed yourself self-medicating in any of the common ways mentioned in this chapter... food, alcohol, sex, drugs, binge-watching TV, work? What might you be willing to make more interesting in your life that will shift your unhealthy habits to healthy ones?

3. What, if any, may have been a possibility for a new pathway in your life that you haven't acted on in the past? Does that possibility still interest you? Are you willing to take the steps to bring that possibility into physical reality?

CHAPTER TWO

How Consciousness Works

"Temporary discomfort pales in the face of long-term awakening." —Alan Cohen

We may have heard it said that "life is consciousness;" yet, do we really know what consciousness means? I have heard individuals use the terms consciousness and awareness interchangeably; yet, I see them as two separate ideas. Awareness is that of which I am currently mindful. Consciousness is the sum total of all my awarenesses.

My awareness can change in the moment, based on my understanding of a current experience. My consciousness expands with each new awareness. I get to choose which awareness I want to continue to be part of my consciousness. Then, what I choose to hold in my consciousness becomes part of the collective consciousness, or consciousness of the human race.

A friend recently asked me, "Can you delete an awareness from your consciousness?" What a really great question! I asked her, "Does hatred exist?" She responded, "Yes." I answered, "It exists at this time, since there are individuals who engage in hating, for whatever reason. However, as each of us makes a conscious decision to no longer engage in hate or look for evidences of it, since it isn't who we are in our heart-of-hearts, we shift our focus to how you and I are on this earth-journey together to lift up each other. The former energy of hate is transformed in our consciousness and begins to dissipate in the collective consciousness as it is replaced with support, inclusion, compassion, Higher Love...unity!

Are there things I don't like? Sure. I don't like anyone to shout at me, for instance; however, I wouldn't hate them if they did. I would let them know in a lowered voice that no one has permission to shout at me. Setting a boundary with individuals sets-up a parameter for what I find acceptable and not acceptable.

Since what I accept as part of my consciousness becomes part of the collective consciousness, it's important for me to be clear about what I do accept. THIS is what is then imprinted in my consciousness, as well as in the consciousness of humanity. Imagine if each of us on the planet were to agree with this concept and eliminate the thought of hatred, since hating anyone would no longer be an option for us? It's been said that nature abhors a vacuum. In shifting the mental and emotional energy away from hatred, what might we be willing to shift to in order to fill the vacuum with a mental and emotional energy that supports Higher Love? May I suggest: kindness, support, understanding, acceptance, inclusion, compassion, encouragement. I'm sure you get the picture.

It takes just one of us to begin a new concept and incorporate it in our daily activities, being the example for others to emulate, if they so choose.

The Hundreth Monkey Effect

There is a story told, hypothetically, about scientists working on an island in the Pacific Ocean, observing the habits and patterns of monkeys living on the island. At one point they observed a female monkey taking a sweet potato, which is a staple in their eating habits, down to the water and washing it before she ate it. Day after day she took her sweet potato to the water, washed it, then ate it. Other monkeys began noticing her new pattern and began washing their sweet potatoes in the water before eating them.

When a majority of monkeys on that island were consistently washing their sweet potatoes before eating them, the scientists observed that monkeys on other islands, even though they had no physical contact with the original monkeys, were also washing their sweet potatoes before eating them. When critical mass was achieved, the practice became part of the monkey consciousness and has been called "The Hundreth Monkey Effect."

Questions to ponder...

1. Have you had difficulty setting boundaries with individuals to communicate what is acceptable to you and what is not? In what way?

2. What is one new way you are willing to show-up in your life that respects who you are as an individual and respectfully communicates the new parameter you have established?

CHAPTER 3

The Conscious/Sub-Conscious Areas Of Mind

"When you rule your mind, you rule your world."
- (Music and lyrics by Bill Provost)

In understanding the way consciousness works, I like to use a visual that I first learned in 1981, while continuing my studies at Unity School for Religious Studies, formerly called Unity Institute for Continuing Education. Through the years, I have added to this visual as my understanding has expanded.

Imagine a cylinder - perhaps an empty can or oatmeal box, laying on its side, with the top and bottom cut off. See Figure 1.

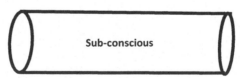

Figure 1: Belief System

Let the inside area of the cylinder represent the sub-conscious area of our one mind. It is in this area that everything we believe to be true is held.

In Figure 2, the left opening of the cylinder represents the conscious area of our mind, which looks out to the physical world of form for input. It then determines what will be retained as a belief in the sub-conscious area, or Belief System (B.S.) I like to include these initials in my explanation, since there have been times when I realized that, in my belief system, I had held on to some b.s. (bull droppings) which were just not true, yet this belief really messed with my understanding of life. More on this idea to follow...

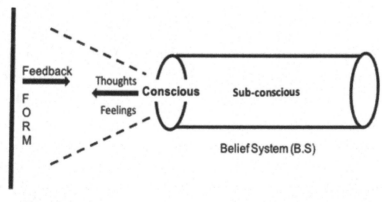

Figure 2

From the left opening, dotted lines are drawn from each side of the cylindrical opening to infinity, symbolizing that the physical world of form cannot be contained or limited. There is an infinite number of forms which can be created in the physical. They are all in potential, waiting to be made visible and usable. Just consider, for a moment, that out of 88 keys on a piano, there has been a plethora of music written in all genres, with much more to come, according to the mind of the composers.

Each of us is composing our lives with each thought, which is then to be followed by an action for the idea to become visible. Remember: no action is also an action. If we are not happy with an outcome, does it benefit us to lash out at the outcome?

If you don't like the movie that's playing on the screen of a particular theater, do you run up and slash the screen or blame the writers or actors or producers? Would you kick in the TV if you didn't like the program? It was a major turn-around in my life when I learned that I'M the writer, producer, director, lead actor, AND the one who draws the cast of characters to play the roles in my production. Skeptical? Okay....read on...

In Figure 2, the solid black line to the left represents an imaginary mirror that reflects back to us the form of the thoughts and feelings we hold, whether consciously or sub-consciously. This is the gift of feedback that life gives us so we may determine whether or not we want to continue to give form to our mind's images.

Have you ever driven to a location, missed your turn, and your surroundings gave you feedback? The first time I drove from Wilkes-Barre to conduct a Sunday Service at Unity in Harrisburg, PA, my husband, knowing that I can be directionally-challenged, told me to simply stay on I-81 south going to the church and on

I-81 north coming home. Simple enough, right? It was March, and there was snow on the sides of the road.

On the way home, which was before GPS days, I followed his directions and drove to I-81 north. I felt very proud of myself! However, I didn't notice the sign that said "I-81 N stay left," and I continued to drive on the same road which stayed I-81 S. My first clue I had missed my turn was the grass was looking greener. Oh, oh! Then I saw the tell-tale sign "Welcome to Maryland!" We still laugh about it. I like to say I "zigged when I should have zagged!"

Our Belief System houses both the fulfilling, endearing, nurturing remembrances of our life experiences, represented by the hearts in figure 3, as well as the regrets, fears, disappointments, resentments, etc., represented by what I like to call squigglies.

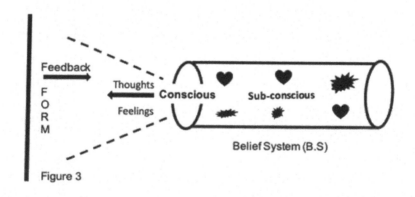

Figure 3

Whatever our conscious area of mind chooses to retain as a belief about ourselves and life is held in the sub-conscious area, or Belief System. At a later time, our understanding of something we had believed was less than loving may be expanded to take in a larger picture.

For example, we may have been passed over for a promotion or even let go from a position at work. We may have felt devalued, unappreciated. As we returned to the job market in search of another position, we may have interviewed for and offered an even better position at a more lucrative salary. We then realize that this blessing in disguise could not have happened if we hadn't "lost" our previous job. I like to see this situation as having been released to greater good.

If we are not willing to shift out of a belief in being a victim, seeing something as unfair, carrying hurt, anger, regret, etc., this less than loving mind energy exacerbates the squigglie already imprinted on our belief system. It reinforces the original victim conclusion and, in the human need to be right, looks for additional evidence to reinforce this conclusion. It becomes a round-robin. The conclusion is reinforced, and the mind looks for and finds more evidence to prove that we're right—we're a victim.

AND THE DRAMA BEGINS...

Since time exists only in the physical, these squigglies may be retained in our Belief System for more than one chapter in our one on-going life experience. Might this be why we may find ourselves, at times, in unpleasant situations that seem to come out of the blue, with no apparent rationale?

It's at times like these our soul's journey has called the cast of characters together to play-out the roles necessary for us to choose how we will now play our role in the production. Life always gives us a second chance to make another first choice. Really?

Heraclitus said, "You can't step in the same river twice." The river is always moving, changing. It's not the same river into which you previously stepped. Life is ever changing. We are ever changing. I'm not the same person I was last week or even yesterday. When I change what I believe about myself, what I believe about others, and what I believe about life, in general, I have another opportunity to use my free will to choose differently.

Sometimes when you've not seen someone in a while, and when you see them again, they may seem so changed you hardly recognize them. Their mannerisms, attitude, their very presence may seem so different. In this now moment you and I can make a new choice about how we're willing to show-up for ourselves and for each other—for the first time!

When a situation has already been created to an uncomfortable, perhaps even painful, dynamic, why not use it to our advantage and be willing to heal it this time around! If the learning is postponed, it will be recreated in another chapter of our on-going life experience. We are born into this "chapter" with no memory of the previous encounter. It is our opportunity to use our gift of free will. We are not limited to our past choices, no matter how many chapters ago they may have taken place.

Being willing to make a loving, healthier choice now, in this moment, frees up the energy we had previously misdirected in unloving ways: anger, hurt, frustration, resistance,,, you get the picture. This same energy can now be available to be reused to produce what we do want to enjoy.

AND THEN THERE WAS...

Many years ago there was a woman in my ministry who provided me with this perfect example. I will call her "Joan." Whenever Joan walked into the church, I felt myself cringe inside, yet I didn't know why. Just hearing her voice in the common area, I wanted to lock myself in my office. At one point Joan even told my husband she felt she had been his mother in a previous chapter. My husband was pleasant to Joan yet didn't go out of his way to be in her company.

At that time I had a friend named Robin who had been a nun. Some years before, after having had a deep meditative experience in a group meditation, Robin realized she had the gift of being able to intuitively perceive experiences from another person's past that may be having either a positive or an adverse effect on their current life situation.

Robin was also able to "see" about six months into the future and share a possible outcome. Of course, this was frowned upon by her Order, so she left the Order to support others to heal.

In one of our sessions together I briefly told Robin about my dissonant feelings toward Joan, without mentioning her name or any of the circumstances. Robin proceeded to share her impressions with me. As Robin saw it, my current husband Bob and I had also been married in a previous chapter. Joan was, indeed, Bob's mother, and she didn't like the fact that he had married me and was no longer with her.

Joan made it her business to create situations where she wanted Bob to choose her over me. Since Bob loved us both and was unwilling to make that choice, he left us both, and I never forgave her!

Having that information created an opening in my mind and in my heart. That night in my own meditation, I asked Spirit to take me back into the remembrance of that chapter. I imagined the three of us, Bob, Joan and me, together in a small circle. I told her we both loved her, and I forgave her. There was a palpable exchange of Higher Love energy among us, in which I basked for a few moments. It felt so real, so present moment.

When I came out of the meditation, I felt a clarity and a lightness that was beyond anything I had previously experienced. I knew, without a doubt, forgiveness had been completed, which changed the energy from that chapter, through any subsequent chapters, and into the present.

The next night I was working late at the church, after having taught an evening class. The doorbell rang at 10 p.m.! I could see through the window that it was Joan! I was surprised and grateful to feel that there was no cringing going on inside me. When I opened the door, Joan said she was driving down the street, saw the light on in my office, and felt compelled to stop in, although she didn't know why. Well, I knew why!

I invited Joan in and shared with her my experience from the session with Robin and from my meditation. We hugged, tears flowed, and Joan had one comment: she said she KNEW she had been Bob's mother at one time! We had a good laugh together, and we have been good friends since that time. The experience certainly reinforced my belief in having unhealed situations from previous chapters recreated in a current chapter to create the potential for a healing.

Who knows how many other possibilities were presented to me in other chapters that I hadn't followed through with. The important point is that the situation became so uncomfortable that I was willing to do whatever was mine to do to disconnect from this tethered, unhealed situation.

The cord was cut, so to speak. Joan went on to play a different role in my life, one that brought about many blessings that shaped my ongoing spiritual direction, for which I am grateful.

Questions to ponder...

1. Have you noticed any feedback from your life's mirror that resembles any b.s. in your B. S. (Belief System?)

2. Was there a time in your life that revealed something you thought was unfair to be a blessing in disguise?

3. Has there been a role-player in your life who brought up some squigglies that you are now willing to see differently? In what way?

CHAPTER 4

A Look At The Soul

"Sorrow looks back. Worry looks around.
Faith looks up."—Ralph Waldo Emerson

Charles Fillmore, co-founder of Unity with his wife Myrtle, referred to the conscious/sub-conscious area of mind as "soul." Fillmore taught, "Soul makes the body; the body is the outer expression of the soul." (Revealing Word, pg. 182, published by Unity School) As I had previously noted, in addition to the physical body being the outer expression of the soul, I also include the body of our affairs. This encompasses our relationships, wellness, prosperity, etc., as an outer expression of whatever we're holding in our soul, or conscious and sub-consciousness parts of the mind.

There is a study called *A Course in Miracles* which refers to the conscious/sub-conscious area as the separate mind we created

23

since we thought we needed one. This is a study that was scribed by Helen Schucman in the late 1970s and published by the Foundation for Inner Peace. This study was another one of the road signs on my journey that highlighted my path to rediscovering the purpose and meaning of all life.

There is no set number of times that we may have an opportunity to choose again, which is one of the major teachings of A Course in Miracles. The opportunities will continue to present themselves until we've finally healed and transformed each squigglie into another heart in our sub-conscious. I believe, each time the opportunity presents itself, the dynamic may seem more intense!

REINFORCING THE CONCEPT

I was once serving in a position where I was not in agreement with how the one in charge was showing-up in their role as spiritual leader. Others who were also in the organization were feeling attacked, hurt, not served. The Sunday Services seemed more like an AA meeting. I experienced an out-of-balance feeling in me, so I went into prayer for guidance. I knew very clearly that the most loving thing I could do in support of the ministry would be to bless it and move on, to serve in a different arena.

I was lovingly welcomed into a new ministry and was very happy teaching classes, offering spiritual counseling, and serving on Sundays when the minister was not available. I also continued my spiritual studies, earning my Licensed Unity Teacher certification.

Despite all the drama, Bob and I made a decision to tithe to the first ministry for six months after leaving.

We also gave the same amount as a gift to the second ministry and prospered doubly. The Prosperity principles DO work. Within 6 months after Bob and I left, about 25 other people also chose to leave.

In the Fall of 1986 I received a call to attend a special meeting since the spiritual leader of the first ministry had accused me of undermining her ministry by leaving and teaching elsewhere. The minister from the second ministry was also called to attend since he had been the sponsor for the first minister. In the meeting I was asked if I was "willing to be crucified?" What did that mean?

I knew I no longer wanted to be affiliated with the leadership in the first ministry. The energy was not in alignment with my vision of ministry and its service to the congregation. Yet, in the meeting I was told to go back and serve in the first ministry, to help them get re-established, since my classes were well-attended. I adamantly resisted, firmly letting it be known that it was my choice alone where I wanted to serve. I did not want to be swayed by group pressure.

When I went home from the meeting, my whole energy felt SO out-of-balance that I laid, face-down, on my bedroom floor and sobbed. I prayed for guidance as to what was mine to do. In my prayer I said "let me shut-up so I can hear the Voice of Wisdom inside me." I got very quiet as I continued to lay on the floor and, in the biblical "twinkling of an eye," I knew the answer with my whole being. I was to call the first minister the next day and offer to do what I didn't want to do in the first place! My whole energy shifted, and I felt calm and centered, eager to take the action I had previously resisted. I became willing, not needing to know the outcome. It was certainly a place of empowerment for me!

I stayed focus on the words of Francis of Assisi, "Wear the world as a loose garment." The minister welcomed my call and asked me to conduct a Prosperity workshop first. I shared my guidance to offer a workshop on non-resistance first, in the hopes that it would bring back others who had left the ministry. This would be presented as my gift to the ministry, and she agreed. The second workshop was to focus on Prosperity principles, with the income from each subsequent presentation being shared between me, as the teacher, and the ministry.

That summer I presented five workshops and conducted three Sunday Services, all without compensation. Through that time there were no thank-you calls or notes offered. I sent a thank-you note for the opportunity to be of service because it was me who was fulfilling a promise I had made to the universe.

The following October I attended the annual regional conference. I learned in the first evening that the ministry had a special meeting that afternoon to incorporate and had declared bankruptcy in the same meeting. The appearance may have been that they were lacking funds to keep the ministry going. There are other reasons for a life situation to appear bankrupt: lack of love, lack of good communication skills, and, especially, lack of appreciation for others. We receive what we give out.

Many years later I received a phone call from the first minister, asking for my forgiveness, and saying "I know now that it wasn't you, it was me." I shared with her one of the basic teachings from A Course in Miracles: "You owe me nothing but love; I owe you nothing but love." Love brings a situation full-circle. It brings it to completion.

Love brings us to a more-expanded perspective, a higher octave, where we may find ourselves in what appears to be a similar situation. The difference is that we are now looking at it from a detached perspective, non-resistantly, staying in our heart-space and not allowing any former squigglie-energy to intrude. We're calling the experience to a higher vibration and imprinting the lesson gleaned into our Belief System for future reference.

The situation will come up again. That's a given. There will be different role players, yet the opportunity to show-up from our heart-space will be a choice that becomes more natural for us each time.

We're "wearing the world as a loose garment," not bound by any constrictions from past choices or the opinions of others.

Questions to ponder...

1. May there have been a time when resistance to following a Higher path kept you in regret? Briefly recall it here...

2. In what way might you respond to a similar situation from your point of understanding today?

CHAPTER 5

A New Look At Evil

"The first rule is to keep an untroubled spirit.
The second is look things in the face
and know them for what they are."
—Marcus Aurelius

There is a song written by Bill Provost, which I mentioned at the beginning of Chapter 3: "When You Rule Your Mind, You Rule Your World." In the song is this line, "Think good, for there is no evil in the world, unless you think there ought to be." Is there evil in the world? What is evil? Let's look at it from a different perspective than what the world sees.

We spell the word E-V-I-L. Now bring to mind the concept of the mirror reflection from Chapter 2. The thoughts and feelings we send out from our conscious/sub-conscious area of mind are reflected back to us from the mirror called "feedback." This is an immeasurable gift from the universe which gives us a glimpse of what we're holding in our belief system.

If I write the word E V I L on a card and hold it in front of a mirror, what is reflected back to me is L-I-V-E. So, EVIL is LIVE - backwards. To me, living backwards is making the outer world more important than our inner being. It's putting more focus on the result than on the action that produced the result.

We realize, or see with real-eyes, and live from the awareness that there is nothing lacking in life. There is nothing to get in the outer that we don't already have within us. We, also, realize that the bottom line is about expressing, rather than getting. This realization keeps us in balance. It supports us to live from a mind-set that is creating the empowering ideas which produce that which blesses and prospers us, as we take action on the ideas.

IS THERE A DEVIL?

We can follow the same example we used for E-V-IL with the word D-E-V-I-L. Print it on a card and hold it up to the mirror. What we see reflected back is L-I-V-E-D! Our past unhealthy choices, all the ways we've lived before this moment that didn't support a healthy lifestyle, come back to tempt us to re-make the same choices. After all, they're familiar, even though they may not have produced the results we wanted.

How many of us have used Flip Wilson's words "the DEVIL that made me do it" to deflect accountability and blame a nonexistent character for our actions? There comes a time in each of our lives when we are called higher in the way we relate to life. Shifting out of this out-worn concept of a mythical figure tempting us, changes the outcome, as we consider what it is we do want to produce.

Did you notice that I didn't say "what we want to create?" The idea of what we want in our life has already been created, or we wouldn't have a concept we wanted to experience it. The key now is taking action to produce it by giving thanks for it in advance and taking the steps to bringing the vision into our life experience.

THE LAW OF MIND ACTION

There is a simple and immutable principle taught by Unity that applies here. It's called "The Law of Mind Action = thoughts held in mind produce after their kind."

Our thoughts, and accompanying feelings about them, will always be projected onto our own particular feedback mirror and not on someone else's mirror. Others receive feedback from their own mirrors, even though individuals unaware of this principle may tend to blame others for their seeming misfortune. Can what's being projected by you have an impact in my life? It can, to the degree that reflects my thoughts and feelings about it!

What action can I take to keep my mental and emotional energy in balance while a situation around me may seem out of control? As I like to say, "Love the H.E.L.L. out of it!" "Hold

Energy of Love and Light!" Each of us is responsible for the thought-energy we're projecting into life. There can be no denying our respective accountability since the feedback is taking place in our own lives.

I'm an original "Trekkie" and would occasionally use scenes from the original Star Trek episodes in my classes the way my good Jewish friend Jesus used parables. Holding an energy of Higher Love in our awareness acts like the force shields on the Starship Enterprise. When an enemy attack was threatening the Starship, Captain Kirk would say to Mr. Spock, "Up shields!" These shields were impenetrable and kept everyone safe inside the Starship. Higher Love is not of this world and is the buffer that helps us to maintain our inner peace, regardless of circumstances in the outer.

Let's remember that our holding a thought and feeling energy of Higher Love doesn't mean we agree with and accept the actions of someone who is behaving in an unloving manner. It means that we empower ourselves to consciously respond to the situation, rather than unconsciously reacting with a similar unloving attitude. We move closer to mastering our energy level, which sets the vibration of the energy we're projecting into life.

To answer the question is there evil in the world, I would respond it's a fact there are people in the world, at this time, who commit acts that are unloving. They act out of a belief that life is about getting and taking and manipulating and having control, rather than about giving and sharing and being kind. They are unaware they hold the master key and can use their thoughts in a way that brings about a new way of living. This is really a sign of strength and inner control they may have thought they needed to show in an outer way to be successful.

GOING BEYOND THE LAW OF MIND ACTION

There is a Law that transcends the Law of Mind Action, and that's the Law of Grace. Grace is the unearned gift of Higher Love. It goes beyond deservability! It can't be earned, even though individuals for millennia have endeavored to please an anthropomorphic God, or God with human qualities, and earn the gift of Grace.

An example I like to use in my classes is to imagine you are a child, and your Dad comes to you and says "I love you so much, I want to give you this gift." You say, "Gee, thanks so much, Dad, and I'll do the dishes and clean my room." Your Dad says, "That's fine, honey; however, I'm giving you this gift." And you say "And I'll mow the lawn and sweep the driveway."

Does this sound familiar? Have we endeavored to make bargains to earn a gift that's been given freely and lovingly to us? I know that I used to ascribe to this line of thinking at one time. There comes a time in our spiritual growth when we step away from the begging and beseeching and bargaining in prayer, and simply open our minds and hearts and give thanks in advance that whatever we're asking for is already ours. Making this shift in our awareness brings a freedom and an empowerment that supports us to rise to a new level of relating to life and, especially, to each other.

As we begin to use the master key of the Law of Mind Action and pay attention to the feedback mirrored back to us, we can and do successfully shift the quality and direction of our thought processes. Each time we live from mindfulness and take responsibility for the energy we're projecting into the space around us, we insure a higher personal quality of life as the guaranteed result.

Our uplifted consciousness uplifts the collective consciousness to the same degree. This then impacts the lives of each individual currently on the planet, as well as those yet to incarnate on the planet, since consciousness never dies. It does change, according to the changes that occur in our individual consciousness.

It's much the same as a pebble thrown into a pool of water. The ripples continue ad infinitum, even though we are no longer able to see them, since the vibration continues energetically. Consciousness is a mind-energy that ripples beyond any human boundaries and energetically impacts lives, just as a small leaf on the water would be impacted by the ripples from the pebble tossed into the water.

The value of being mindful and consciously choosing the quality of our thoughts, feelings, words, and actions is immeasurable! The more we practice mindfulness the less conscious action will be required since the practice will establish a pattern of conscious living that represents who we really are in our heart of hearts.

Questions to ponder...

1. The appearance of E V I L in the outer can bring up thoughts and feelings of anguish or fear of attack. In what way might you empower yourself to rise above the appearance when a situation seems out of control?

2. What does "love the H.E.L.L. out of a person or situation" look like to you?

3. If you've used a beseeching and bargaining tactic in prayer in the past, in what way are you now willing to shift your approach to prayer?

CHAPTER SIX

The Super-Conscious Area Of Mind

"Do you want to know the difference between a master and a beginner? The master has failed more times than the beginner has ever tried!" —Yoda

Contrary to worldly belief, there is more to our mind than the conscious and sub-conscious areas. In furthering our studies, our understanding expands to include the super-conscious area of mind, which is what I believe my good Jewish friend Jesus referred to as the kingdom of the heavens. This phrase is translated from the Greek word Ouranos, as "realm of expanded awareness."

This realm is designated on the following diagram by drawing dotted lines from the right side of the cylindrical opening, which mirror the ones on the left side. Just as the conscious mind looks outward to the never-ending expanse of physical possibilities, the super-conscious area of mind looks within to the never-ending depth of infinite ideas. It is the non-physical space from which the Ideas of all things in potential evolve. See figure 4

It is important to note here that the sub-conscious area is pivotal. It has the capacity to look to and receive input from the physical world of form through the conscious mind. It can, also, pivot toward the super-conscious area, as we direct our attention within in times of introspection, contemplation, prayer and meditation.

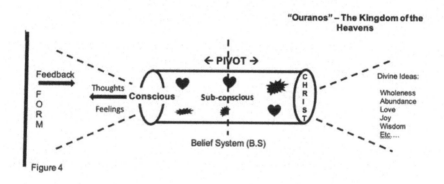

Figure 4

A LESSON FROM BROTHER LAWRENCE

There was a French Christian monk named Brother Lawrence (1614 – 1691) who served as a lay brother in a Carmelite monastery in Paris. He is commonly remembered for the intimacy he expressed concerning his relationship to his understanding of God. His practice was compiled in a little book after his death, which is known as The Practice of the Presence of God. His practice was simply to do whatever was his to do as an act of loving service so that his experience of the Presence was one of the highest vibrations of Love of which he was capable of experiencing... at that time.

TUNING TO CONCERT PITCH

When I think of a vibration, I think of an instrument like a piano that has been tuned to what is called concert pitch. On a piano, which is my favorite instrument and one on which I have been trained, concert pitch is A440.000 c.p.s., or cycles per second. This means that, when tuning a piano, the A key above middle C is tuned to a vibration of 440 cps. Then all the other keys are tuned to match the vibration of this key. It's usually played by the oboe when the instruments are tuning up before a concert.

When the members of the orchestra return for the second-half of the concert, the oboist, once again, plays this pitch so that the other instruments, especially the stringed instruments, may recheck the vibration of their strings, which affects the pitch.

Here's where I find it helpful in my daily routine to stop and check the vibration of my heart-strings, if my energy feels off-balance. Have I been sending out the highest vibration of love of which I am capable, so that I may experience the fullness of Unconditional Love returned to me?

Actually, I'm always sending out the highest vibration of love of which I am capable at that time, depending on the state of my mind and heart at-that-time! And the good news is...No one and no thing can prevent me from shifting my state of mind and heart. If I have, consciously or unconsciously, allowed any squigglies to set-up an unbalanced energy within me, I have the capacity to re-tune to concert-pitch.

It's a simple act...stop and breathe, which quickens the vibration being directed through me, as the instrument through which I experience, and influence, life. My concert pitch is the O.B.O.E. (Original Breath of Energy) within me. The bottom line is... the more I follow-through with my intention to be a bringer of light and love right where I am, the richer and fuller is my experience of the Presence...the Presence of Wholeness...of Fulfillment...of Joy...of Oneness with all Life.

GOING BEYOND CONCERT PITCH

Mind which, in referring to our previous analogy, would be a vibration beyond 440 cps since It is unlimited. Just as our ideas are created by our mind according to our understanding, what is already created in Divine Mind are Divine Ideas. These Divine Ideas are the highest integrity of all ideas... the perfect pattern of all forms that can potentially be produced in the physical. The actual outcome of these ideas in the physical is according to the awareness—the understanding - of the one doing the producing. For example, let's say a building is contracted to be erected. The contractor has a pattern, a blueprint, to use for the ideal construction to be completed as originally planned. If the contractor doesn't follow the pattern, or uses sub-standard materials, the end result will not be the ideal creation that was in potential to be built. I trust this example clarifies the idea.

These Divine Ideas are present AS the fullness of all the qualities of All-Good inherent in the Presence. They have no other purpose than to be experienced in their Fullness in the physical dimension. If I, as the producer in my life, use stinkin' thinkin', as it's been called, letting the squigglies, the regrets, blames, etc., filter into my use of these ideas, the result will be less than healthy, abundant, harmonious, fulfilling.

The more our mind functions from this raised vibration of Higher Love, we naturally and consistently produce the form of these ideas in the physical. We complete our purpose to bring the Kingdom of the Heavens, the realm of expanded awareness, on the Earth.

MORE THAN ENOUGH

We are being called to live mindfully in the awareness that all possibilities exist for everyone on the planet, at all times and in all places, not withholding any good from any individual. As we do, we open the potential for everyone on the planet, who is willing to live in this awareness, to bring these ideas into physical form. There is more than enough for everyone to use, share, and enjoy. So then...why don't we experience these qualities in our lives on a consistent basis?

In the Book of Genesis, chapter 1, in the Hebrew Scripture we read that the first creation was light... "Let there be Light."

This realm of expanded awareness, the super-conscious area, is filled with Light. This Light represents the fullness of all the Divine Ideas present and readily available for our use.

LET THERE BE LIGHT

Imagine this Light like a flashlight with its beam pointed through the cylinder in our diagrams from the super conscious, through the sub-conscious, in the direction of the physical world of form. As the light travels, first through the sub-conscious area, it encounters all the hearts and squigglies we've accepted as part of our Belief System.

My Dad was an amateur photographer and loved to take movies of my two sisters and me, have them put onto a film reel, then show the movies from his projector onto his movie screen. Whenever the projector light was on and there was no film on the movie reel, my sisters and I enjoyed using our fingers to produce shadows which appeared as images like rabbit ears or other animals in front of the light. These shadows then showed-up on the screen. The screen gave us feedback to show us what we had placed in the path of the light.

This concept is the same in our minds. The Light that is at the center of each of us in our super-conscious area is always radiating outward. This light moves through our sub-conscious and our conscious areas on its path to the outer world of physical form. As it does, it picks up the images of whatever beliefs we've accepted in our sub-conscious that we believe are the truth about ourselves.

SMALL *"t"* OR CAPITAL *"T"*

I see anything that is perceived as less-than-good as a small 't' truth, which changes as my value of it changes. The super-conscious area holds the capital 'T' Truths that are permanent and are consistently available to experience on demand. As a result, the image it projects onto the screen of our lives appears as either the hearts - love, wellness, harmony, etc., or the squigglies - the appearance of scarcity, illness, inharmony, doubt, or other appearances of lack or incompleteness that we saw in figure 3.

Yes... our screen of life mirrors back to us the projections of whatever obstacles we have placed in the path of the Light. These obstacles have, and are, producing the appearance of shadows in our lives. It would be the same as if we had an x-ray taken of our sub-conscious. Any squigglies, or obstacles, would show up as a shadow on the x-ray.

Our willingness to be aware of any resentments, unhealthy attitudes and behaviors, and other ways we may have disrespected our inherent value supports us in our new willingness to shift our focus. Instead, we make loving attitudes and healthy behaviors more important than the resentments, etc. We love ourselves into transforming the energy of squigglies into the clear, transparent energy of love, compassion, and support - hearts! Any shadows are eliminated, and we are now free to enjoy the resulting harmony and wellness.

Questions to ponder...

1. Has there been a time in your life when "stinkin' thinkin'" got in the way of bringing a raised vibration of Higher Love into your life? In what way might you have moved beyond it?

2. If squigglies of regret, resentment, etc. are
still messing with your enjoyment of a free flow of harmony and wellness, what action are you willing to take to release the need to hold on to the squigglie energy which is holding your good hostage?

3. Is there anyone you might be, consciously or unconsciously, exempting from the thought of greater good, labeling them as unworthy? If so, are you now willing to open the channel of greater good in your own life by holding a vision of worthiness for each person, no matter the outer appearance?

CHAPTER SEVEN

Moving Into Action

"Do not take life's experiences too seriously. Above all, do not let them hurt you, for in reality they are nothing but dream experiences...
If circumstances are bad
and you have to bear them,
do not make them a part of yourself.
Play your part in life,
but never forget that it is only a role."
—Paramahansa Yogananda

It is universally-known and taught by master teachers from many philosophies that there is no lack of any good thing, as we live out of the awareness of the Presence of All-Good. So, now it's time to move from willingness into action. This may beg the question, "how do I shift out of this place in life that may feel incomplete so that I, too, may enjoy this Fullness that is said to be my potential?"

And the answer is...One thought at-a-time. In the words of Viktor E. Frankl, neurologist and psychiatrist in the early 1900s who survived various Nazi concentration camps, from his book Man's Search For Meaning, "Between stimulus and response there is a space. In that space is our power to choose our response. In our response lies our growth and our freedom."

In our search for meaning and purpose in life we encounter a myriad of opportunities to choose again...to use this new awareness we've been discussing to gain clarity and a sense of centeredness. In this way, like Frankl, our responses come from a renewed place of mental, emotional, and spiritual growth. We give ourselves permission to respond out of the super-conscious area of our mind where we may access the readily available ideas that resonate at a higher vibration.

These ideas, while readily available, will never force themselves into our awareness. In the Book of Revelation (3:20) we read, "Behold, I stand at the door and knock. If any man opens the door, I will come in and sup with him and he with me."

WHAT IS NEW THOUGHT CHRISTIANITY

Standing at the entrance of our super-conscious area of mind is what New Thought Christianity, which includes the Unity teachings, refers to as "the Christ." New Thought Christianity is a movement which began in the late 1800s and consists of a group of religious denominations, authors, philosophers, and individuals who share a set of beliefs concerning metaphysics, positive thinking, creative visualization, and healing. It holds that Infinite Intelligence, or God, is everywhere present, divinity dwells within each person, and all people are spiritual beings, learning through this human experience, The highest spiritual principle is loving another unconditionally, and what we think becomes our experience in daily living.

The term Christ comes from the Greek word "Christos," which means the Anointed One. The Christ is the ideal pattern in which humankind, in all its life forms, is created. Traditional Christianity teaches that Christ refers only to Jesus of Nazareth.

New Thought Christianity teaches that this ideal pattern was modeled for us by Jesus of Nazareth, as he showed us how to live a life of nonresistance. Jesus is seen as our brother and way-shower. Our Jewish friends might call this ideal "The Jehovah," which is the counterpart of the Christ Similarly, our Buddhist friends may see this ideal pattern as "The Buddha."

Each one of us is an Anointed One, no matter what our spiritual tradition, or absence of one, may be. Each of us is the Christ, at our level of understanding, with the potential to more fully express our divine potential as we refine our understanding to be aware of even the slightest shift in our centeredness.

I might dare to contrast the Christ-level of understanding with a human level by noting the difference between someone at a doctorate level and a kindergartener. Yet, it's important for a teacher at a doctorate level to use terms in teaching that would, first, connect with a kindergartener's understanding. They would, then, be more responsive to being brought to a more-expanded understanding right where they are...identifying colors, counting, learning the alphabet. This is what Jesus did with the people in his day, using parables about what they could comprehend.

It's important for us, also, to meet people at a shared level of understanding in our interactions, not talking up or down to others, and respecting whatever place they are on their spiritual path.

FROM REEL TO REAL

The Greek word "ecclesia" means the "called-out ones" and is used in references to "church." Each of us has been called-out from the worldly belief that the material world is the real world. I see the material world as the reel world...the world of projected images from the minds of humankind. We are called to make the conscious choice to live more mindfully in the awareness of the Presence of All-Good.

In this way we bring that aspect of our Oneness back into the collective Wholeness that isn't complete until each one of us returns to our rightful place in and AS the Presence. We return home via what A Course in Miracles refers to as "the journey without distance to a place that we never left."

OPENING THE DOOR

I see this willingness to open the door to the super-conscious area as the key that unlocks this realm of expanded awareness. I come to realize that I already own and have always had this key available for my use each time I spend time in the stillness of my inner being, no matter the length of physical time. Remember: time only exists in the physical dimension. Living from the super-conscious area is evidence that we have opened the portal referred to as "the Christ" and see this divine potential in ourselves and others.

This supports us in being aware of any past unhealthy choices that are now being presented as an opportunity to choose again. We come to realize that our past choices were not mistakes. They were the best choices we were able to make in the state of awareness we were in at that time. The closer we get to realizing and living from this area of mind, the more pushback we may feel from that aspect of ourselves that wants to remind us of our unworthiness and to challenge us on the audacity of seeing ourselves as the Christ.

Holding ourselves in judgment of having sinned, creates another squigglie in our Belief System, or sub-conscious area, which is why I refer to this idea of S.I.N, as "Self-Inflicted Nonsense."

At each moment of choice, which is every moment, I alone determine what is most important for me to hold in my sub-conscious, as the truth about my life...a small 't' truth, which changes as my value of it changes.

When was the last time you actually looked at the feedback your life was presenting to you? If you have looked at it, might you have wondered why seemingly unloving things were happening to you as a good person? Perhaps you had seen it as God punishing you. Perhaps you thought of it as payback for something less than loving you may have done... in other words, the Buddhist belief in Karma. It has also been seen as what goes around comes around.

In my former Catholic training I would fault myself with a "mea culpa, mea culpa, mea maxima culpa"- through my fault, through my fault, through my most grievous fault."

NO FAULT ASSURANCE

Some years ago I heard a statement that was literally a life-changing experience for me. "How can I fault myself for something I did while I was learning." WOW – that was really an eye-opener for me.

Ask yourself, "Am I willing to see myself as learning through this life experience?" If the answer is "YES," then ask yourself if you would make the same choice with your understanding of today. If the answer is "NO," then why would you continue to fault yourself for something you did while you were learning?

Choose again. Be willing to let go of any regret or guilt. Come into the light of the present moment and give thanks for the freeing gift of grace! This phrase comes up for us time and time again as we come to that fork in the road ... again... and again. We are never limited to our past choices.

In the light of this same understanding, what about all the individuals WE have faulted because of something THEY did? Are we willing to also see them as learning through their life experiences, whether or not it's apparent to us they are willing to learn? What if they do continue in the same behavior? Are we still willing to hold open this space in our minds and hearts and step back in judgment, seeing them as learning through their life's choices, as we have and are, until they are willing to choose again? Are we willing to give EACH individual the space to come up higher in their understanding, just as we would want others to give to us? "How can I fault you for something you did while you were learning?"

Does this mean that we are to forgive others for their less-than-loving behaviors? As I see it, forgiveness is called-for when there has been a judgment - a blame. When there's no judgment, is there a need for forgiveness? Perhaps the forgiveness can be directed toward ourselves for having held the judgment in the first place. This leaves our energy open to a broader understanding which includes compassion.

STOP WAITING FOR FORGIVENESS

Are you waiting for God to forgive you, yet are holding a judgment against yourself? What if I told you you can stop waiting for God to forgive you since there's never been a judgment in the first place. How can Absolute Love judge or hold a condemnation? Be willing to accept the unearned gift of grace and choose again.

Disconnect your energy from the reel world and step into the Real world...a universe parallel to the worldly view, yet devoid of the blame, shame, guilt trips, or other judgments our human mind may tell us is our duty to hold, in order to hold the other person accountable. In the words of Michele Obama, "when they go low, we go high."

A TRIP TO McDONALDS

Whenever I offer a class on relationships, I like to have a conversation with the class that often goes this way...

ME: "How many of you have ever eaten at McDonalds?" Most everyone has.

ME: "How many of you have ever ordered a steak dinner there?"

CLASS: "You can't order a steak dinner at McDonald's."

ME: " Why not?"

CLASS: "They don't serve steak."

ME: "What if I stood on the counter, stomped my feet, and demanded a steak dinner? Would they give it to me?"

CLASS: "No, they don't have it to give."

Have we ever done that in relationships, expecting a "steak dinner" (or rice and lentils in my case, as a vegetarian) yet they just don't have it to give? We either accept the person as they are and look for ways to call the situation higher between us, or we may choose to leave the relationship, if the situation becomes intolerable, as in the case of abuse or addiction.

Here is where receiving guidance from a trained counselor, life coach, minister, or therapist can be invaluable support on our life path. Individuals have also received needed support from 12-

step groups. Being willing to acknowledge we are at an impasse in our lives and are open to support sets the universe in motion. The act of being humble, teachable, shines light on our path and guides us in the appropriate direction. Then, the ball is in our court, to receive and use the guidance, staying awake to the opportunities to choose again.

I like the following quote from Mike Dooley, who writes as the Universe, "When someone behaves poorly, it's always because they've forgotten how powerful they really are, how beautiful life is, and how much they're loved."

IT TAKES PRACTICE

This is a practice that takes practice. There may be times when it may not seem like we, or they, are making much progress, yet - have you ever seen Chinese Bamboo? In its first 4 years after being planted, we can't see any change above the surface. What we don't see is that a massive root structure is forming below ground. In the 5th year the plant climbs from 0 to 80 feet in just one year. Have patience - with yourself and with the people around you. "It works when you work it!"

EXPANSION AND CONTRACTION

With each shift in perception (what A Course in Miracles calls the miracle) we expand our awareness of our super-conscious area of mind and contract the "separate mind we thought we needed." Imagine a collapsible cup that we can expand as we want to use it or contract when it's no longer necessary. This is the idea.

We make the decision to pivot our conscious/sub-conscious area, or soul awareness, away from receiving info from the physical world as real, and we direct it toward the super-conscious area, living from this focus on a more-mindful basis.

We no longer have an investment in the reality, the permanence, of the physical world and allow it to change. Affecting the change is important to the over-all unfolding of our life processes. Mindfully raising-up our thoughts to a higher vibration, we begin to contract the conscious/sub-conscious area of mind until it returns to the nothingness from which it came. We no longer have a use for this area of mind since we are fulfilling our purpose of living from the super-conscious area!

We reclaim our divine identity as a Christed-being, entitled to bring forth this greater Good onto the stage of life, even in the face of disaster or calamity...even a pandemic. We are living from our True Nature, the super-conscious, the "kingdom of the heavens," and are thereby creating this new stage of life "on Earth as it is in Heaven."

Questions to ponder...

1. What might you have accepted as the truth about yourself that you now realize is a small 't" truth? In what way are you willing to define yourself that now validates the capital "T" Truth about you?

2. Is there a judgment you had placed on yourself that you are now willing to release since seeing it as a choice you made while you were learning? In what way are you willing to see yourself differently?

3. Has there been a judgment you placed on another person that you are now willing to release since seeing it as a choice they made whle they were learning? In what way are you willing to see them differently?

PART TWO

THE TRINITY:
WHAT IS IT?

CHAPTER EIGHT

What Is The Trinity?

"Live in the present. Launch yourself on each wave,
find eternity in each moment..."
—Henry David Thoreau

This brings us to our discussion on the Trinity. What is the general concept of the Trinity? Generally, it's understood that the trinity is three in one. Whether it's in our human selves, our spiritual selves, or a religious concept. it all involves three aspects in one.

THE HUMAN TRINITY

Let's begin with the Human Trinity - three aspects of each human, symbolized in Figure 5. Represented at the apex is Spirit, or super-conscious area of our mind. At the left angle is soul, or the conscious / sub-conscious area, with the body and the body of our affairs positioned at the lower right angle. These three aspects are all present in each one of us.

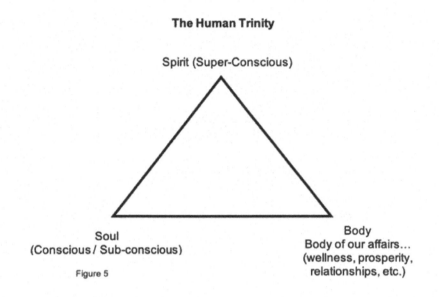

The Human Trinity

Spirit (Super-Conscious)

Soul
(Conscious / Sub-conscious)

Body
Body of our affairs...
(wellness, prosperity,
relationships, etc.)

Figure 5

THE TRINITY IN TRADITIONAL CHRISTIANITY

The concept of the Christian Trinity is one I learned growing up in the Catholic faith in the 1940s and '50s. We were told by both the priests and the nuns, who taught in the parochial school I attended, there was no logical explanation for the Trinity. You were simply to accept it on faith and, as a child, I did and believed it for many years.

According to Wikipedia, "The Trinity is a Christian conception of God as consisting of three persons – the Father, the

Son, and the Holy Spirit – sharing the same substance." Substance is another word for Nature. See Figure 6. In the Revealing Word, published by Unity School and first printed in 1959, Charles Fillmore teaches, "Father is the source, origin, essence of all. Son is that which proceeds from, is begotten of the Father, like Him in nature, and essentially all that the Father is. Holy Spirit is God's word in movement: the working, moving, breathing of Spirit, made known to men through revelation, inspiration, and guidance...The doctrine of the trinity is often a stumbling block, because we find it difficult to understand how three persons can be one. Three persons cannot be one, and theology will always be a mystery until theologians become metaphysicians."

**The Trinity
in Traditional Christianity**

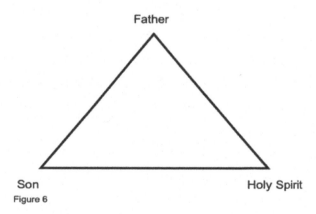

Figure 6

When I resumed my journey as a spiritual seeker in the 1970s, my thirst for a more-expanded understanding of spiritual principles led me to the study of different religions and philosophies. It wasn't until the early 1990s that my mind began to embrace a broader vision of the Christian Trinity, which lifted my understanding to the next level, or octave. The more I listened to my inner voice, the more the veils covering my understanding began to part and the invisible became visible.

This changed the trajectory of both my personal study and my teaching. As a result, this quest drew new teachers and mentors into my life, like Matthew Fox, Eckhart Tolle, Dr. Wayne Dyer, Rev. Jim Rosemergy and so many others. More from Jim Rosemergy in a later chapter.

Another teacher who made a most-profound impact on my understanding was John Shelby Spong. a former Episcopal bishop who has made tremendous inroads in the global spiritual consciousness through his many years of study and teaching. I continue to find myself resonating with Bishop Spong's manner of relaying the depths of his understanding through the many lectures I've attended, books read, and in our personal conversations. Listening to Jack share his wisdom is like "sitting at the feet of the master." I feel very blessed to called Jack and his wife Christine friends.

I devoured Spong's book The Sins of Scripture in two days; each day feeling like I had just eaten a full meal. It really opened my eyes to how understanding the language and customs of the Aramaic people played such a large part in the writing of Scripture.

One of the examples I like to use is found in the Sermon on the Mount, Matthew 5:39, "... whoever strikes you on your right cheek, turn to him the other also."

This passage used to puzzle me, until I understood that "turning the other cheek" is an idiom in the Aramaic language. It means, if you were looking at the situation in one way, with your right cheek forward, turn the other cheek and look at it from a different perspective." We use idioms in our language today, as well..

For example, let's say I wrote a book and told a story about a man who walked into a room and said to his friend "hey man, slap me five." If someone were to pick up that book two thousand years from now, they would, most likely, wonder why the man would ask his friend to slap him five times. Yet, based on today's language and customs, we would understand that the man asked his friend to give him a "high five."

I, also, continue to be grateful for the endearing and enduring friendship and spiritual connection with my friends Rev. Jim Rosemergy and his wife Nancy. Jim's depth of inner wisdom and his ability to impartthis wisdom, even simply by his very presence, is a gift I have treasured since we first reconnected in the physical dimension in 1987. To have been ordained a Unity minister by Jim in 1996 is an added blessing.

THE HEBREW TRINITY

Christianity is an out-growth of Judaism. In the Hebrew

tradition there is no actual teaching of the Trinity. In questioning my good friend, Rabbi Larry Kaplan, he shared that he sees the Trinity from a Hebrew perspective as God (Holiness,) Torah (teaching,) and Israel (place/center.) The Hebrew Trinity, as intuited by me from the Hebrew Scripture, is represented in Figure 7.

The Trinity in Hebrew

Elohim – Let us make man in our image and likeness

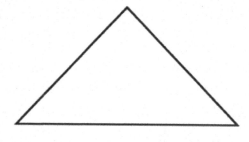

Jehovah (Yehovah)
Creates life forms
Figure 7

Yahveh (YHVH)
Divine Breath moves
Creation into Existence

Elohim, at the apex, is the partnering of the masculine and feminine aspects of the Creator, hence the plural pronoun, as we read in Genesis 1:26, "Then God said, 'let us make man in Our Image, according to Our likeness...'"

The Jehovah (Yehovah,) positioned at the left angle, is the counterpart of the Christ, or Son in Christianity. It is the aspect that does the forming of that which is created in Idea. We read this concept in Genesis 2:7, when the Lord God formed Adam out of the soil of the earth. Then the Yahveh aspect of the Trinity, represented at the right angle, breathes life into creation for it to come into Existence.

The Hebrew alphabet has no vowels, only consonants. The name Yahveh would be Y H V H (Yod Hey Vav Hey.) In an attempt to sound-out the letters YH it might sound like an inhalation, while VH an exhalation. Once again, it's the Divine Breath that brings form into existence!

Questions to ponder...

1. Did your formative years include a teaching of the Trinity which seemed far-removed from your human understanding? Can you articulate it?

CHAPTER NINE

Understanding the Metaphysical Trinity

"It is your mission to express all that you can imagine God to be. Let this be your standard of achievement; never lower it, nor allow yourself to be belittled by the cry of sacrilege. You can attain everything that you can imagine."
—Charles Fillmore, *Talks on Truth*

Our discussion, up to this point, sets the stage for a deeper look into viewing the Trinity from a metaphysical perspective. The term metaphysics is seeing how mind, from the Greek word meta, comes before the physical... or looking beyond the physical.

The metaphysical trinity, as I see it, is outlined in Figure 8 as: Mind, Idea, and Expression. Each of these three aspects symbolizes the Divine characteristic present at each level. Divine Mind is the Source and originator of all ideas. The Divine Idea refers to the Christ -- the ideal pattern out of which every form of life can be produced at its purest integrity. Expression in the physical takes place as Life is breathed into the Idea. The Idea then becomes part of physical creation at the highest level of understanding of the one bringing it into expression.

For example, there is nothing greater than Divine Mind...It is Absolute! This makes the Idea It generates absolute, as well. Divine Mind doesn't have ideas. It IS the ultimate idea of creation that is whole and complete. In the words of Judge Thomas Troward, "Wherever Spirit is at all, the whole of Spirit must be." Spirit is everywhere present at the same time. So, there is not more Spirit present and available in one church or religion than another, or in one country than another, or in one person than another.

The Metaphysical Trinity
Three Aspects of One Source

Divine Mind

The Absolute – The Source of all that is – The Originator of all Divine Ideas

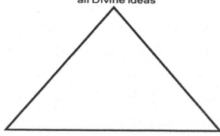

Divine Idea
The Ideal Pattern of the full potential of Creation.

Expression
Divine Breath of Life bringing the Divine Idea from potential to Expression.

Figure 8

TURNING OUR FOCUS UPSIDE DOWN

In viewing the Christian Trinity from a metaphysical perspective, a new understanding can emerge as the position of the triangle is reversed—apex pointing downward and using a dotted line to complete the top outline of the triangle. This dotted line represents Divine Mind, the masculine/feminine, or Father/Mother aspect of the Creator, which is infinite in nature and cannot be contained in form. The area in the center of the triangle represents Divine Idea, or that which is ideated by Divine Mind, the Ideal in potential in physical form.

The downward point of the triangle signifies Spirit, the whole Spirit of God, which meets our human trinity at the point of Spirit, or super-conscious area of our one mind. It is the connecting point where all exists as one.

As a review from our previous discussion in chapter 2, we note that this area of mind, I believe, was referred to by Jesus as the kingdom of the heavens, translated from the Greek word Ouranos, as realm of expanded awareness. See Figure 9.

From this connecting point we draw an upward facing triangle whose apex coincides with the downward facing apex of the top triangle. The center of the lower triangle represents Charles Fillmore's teaching of soul, the conscious/sub-conscious areas of mind. Another dotted line is drawn to complete this triangle, signifying that there is no limit to the physical realm in which form is expressed as our body and the body of our affairs - creativity, wellness, financial prosperity, relationships, etc.

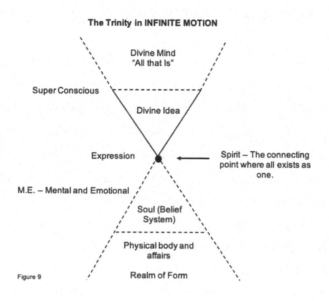

The Trinity in INFINITE MOTION

Divine Mind
"All that Is"

Super Conscious

Divine Idea

Expression ●←— Spirit – The connecting
point where all exists as
one.

M.E. – Mental and Emotional

Soul (Belief
System)

Physical body and
affairs

Figure 9　　　　Realm of Form

ENERGY CONTINUALLY MOVES

The creative energy of Divine Mind is always in infinite motion as it moves into Expression in the physical realm through our spirit, mind, and body!

I had previously stated: in the beginning, humankind thought it needed to create a mind separate from God-Mind, which is a teaching from A Course in Miracles. This belief led to thoughts and feelings of inadequacy, fear and scarcity, since this mind takes its input from appearances in the outer world. As we allow these limiting beliefs to take-up residence in our Belief System, they detract from the Pure Light of Divine Ideas moving through our mind from the super-conscious area.

PAY ATTENTION TO THE FEEDBACK

These limiting beliefs, or squigglies, are then projected onto the screen of life and show-up in our world as the feedback of dis-ease in the physical, or mental/emotional body, or inharmony in relationships, or appearances of lack, etc. This feedback is a powerful tool which offers us an opportunity to re-examine the results of our belief system (B.S.), continually being mirrored onto the screen of life.

It's important to pay attention to the feedback that is presented to us by life and to clear out the limiting thoughts and feelings in our sub-conscious. This frees-up any guilty attachment to what we've believed was a s.i.n., which I have referred to as self-inflicted nonsense. This clearing out creates a vacuum in our mental and emotional energy field (m.e.), our conscious/sub-conscious area of mind.

FILLING THE VACUUM

It's been said that nature abhors a vacuum. Our mind is no different. This area of mind is now ready to consciously shift its focus as we remember that we are spiritual beings, learning and growing through each human experience. We mindfully pivot our focus away from the realm of form and keep our eye single on our oneness with Divine Mind. Each of us IS the Divine Idea ideated by Divine Mind – All That IS. See Figure 10.

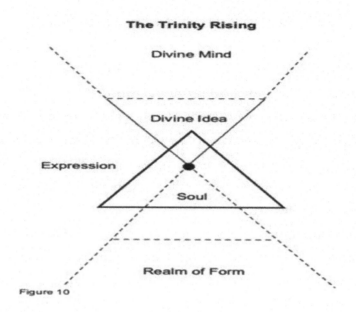

The Trinity Rising

Divine Mind

Divine Idea

Expression

Soul

Realm of Form

Figure 10

With each more loving, or higher, thought and corresponding action in life, we lift up our Human Trinity, body, mind and spirit, into the likeness of our spiritual nature AS the Divine Idea, the Christ. "And I, when I am lifted up from the earth, will draw every man to me." Gospel of John 12:32, Lamsa translation from the Peshitta, the ancient Aramaic version of Scripture. See Figure 11.

In conscious remembrance of our true nature as Pure Spirit, we are now ready to "live and move and have our being" (Acts 17:28) AS the Image-Bearer of All That IS. See Figure 12.

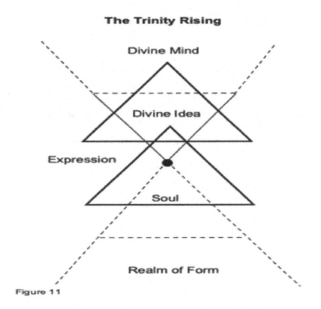

The Trinity Rising

Divine Mind

Divine Idea

Expression

Soul

Realm of Form

Figure 11

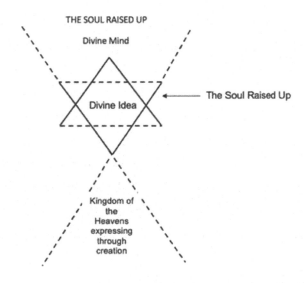

THE SOUL RAISED UP

Divine Mind

Divine Idea ← The Soul Raised Up

Kingdom of
the
Heavens
expressing
through
creation

Figure 12

THE FINAL PIECE OF THE PUZZLE

Figure 12 is the form that was intuited to me in the memorable class so many years ago, as I was sharing with students what I was hearing inside. What we see that has emerged is a Star of David. How ironic! We have seen this symbol for millennia, yet how it relates to our rightful place in the Trinity had not been clear to me until that moment.

RECLAIMING OUR RIGHTFUL PLACE

We come to realize that we have always had a rightful place in the Trinity. We have never been a worm of the dust, or whatever other unworthy labels we may have had put on us. We see with real eyes, and we know that we are being called to put a lifestyle shift into motion. This conscious shift results in our ability to live in the NOW moment.

We experience the direct expression of the All-Good from the super-conscious area of our One-Mind. It is from THIS area that we now impact physical creation.

There is no longer a separate mind that has the potential to thwart the free flow of Divine Ideas, or higher thoughts, into our lives. As we claim it, it is fulfilled. The "it" is whatever you choose it to be. Even small shifts can make a huge impact in our lives and in the lives of others.

Just as we have learned from observing the lives of other Master teachers, others may, also, learn from our example and begin to create the shifts in their own approach to life. One thought-at-a-time...this is the simple, yet sacred, mantra that lights the way to reclaiming our individual and collective rightful place in the Trinity, as the collective Christ...collective Yehovah, collective Buddha...collective Krishna!

I am... YOU are... WE are... the Divine Idea, the Christos... the One more-fully awakening to and being the Truth of our Spiritual Nature.

Questions to ponder...

1. Are there any thoughts and feelings of inadequacy, fear, and/or scarcity you have noticed come to the surface as you pay attention to the feedback in your life?

2. As you consciously pivot your focus away from the physical world, and keep your eye single on that aspect of you that is your spiritual self, is there a noticeable shift that takes place in you as you engage in your life experiences? What does that look like?

Ann Marie Acacio

CHAPTER TEN

Living From Our Rightful Place

"All great souls and spiritual leaders tap a stream of consciousness where all people are brothers and sisters rather than members of a particular religion... When will Christians finally spy the Christ in Moslems who pray five times a day? When will Moslems see the Hidden Imam in the untouchables, harijan, of India? Will the people of the earth understand their own spiritual path so thoroughly that they will see that the Buddha of the Buddhist, the Christ of the Christians, and the Krishna of the Hindus is the same spiritual nature that rests in silent repose in every human being?"—Jim Rosemergy, *The Third Coming*

In our spiritual journey it is important to come to a point where we let go of the words and diagrams and books and classes and set-aside times to simply BE - in the silence. It is what my friend Jim Rosemergy, in his book The Watcher, calls going to the "High

Meadow." It may seem elusive, at first, yet the more we "rest in silent repose," the more this "High Meadow" comes to the forefront of who we are and how we show-up in life.

It is here that we come to experience what my good Jewish friend Jesus referred to in John 17: as being in the world yet not of it. Each time we detach our mental and emotional energy from the world of form, even for an instant, we draw our energy inward. I like to refer to it as my m.e. (mental/emotional) energy since it's who I am as a spiritual being, being human.

We build a treasury of peace-filled experiences on which to draw during those stretching places in our lives. These encounters with other spiritual beings being human on our path through life offer us the opportunity to be honed...to be made more effective. Each life experience brings its own gift we recognize more readily as we become, what I like to call, the sacred witness to life.

A LESSON FROM A CHILDREN'S FAIRY TALE

Just like in the children's fairy tale *The Princess and the Pea*, by Hans Christian Andersen, each of us is the princess whose sensitivity is able to feel the pea under the many "huge mattresses and 20 featherbeds." We can clearly discern when we've allowed our energy to become entangled with any less than loving energy of another person or situation.

We can feel more acutely those times when our energy is out-of-balance. We know that anything that is not in-line with our true nature as a spiritual being must come up to be healed and released! Each of us is birthing a new reality in our lives which then translates to a new reality for our planet. We are playing the role of mid-wife for ourselves and for each other as we support one another in this birthing process.

BEING CALLED TO THE DEAFENING SILENCE

Our whole being is called to the experience of inner S I L E N C E, even in, and especially in, the outer appearance of turmoil. I recently experienced the following, very loudly and clearly, in the aftermath of the 2020 Presidential election. I found my energy being drawn off-center by comments from others, especially family members, and most definitely in the attack on Capitol Hill on January 6, 2021. Being in the midst of and watching the unloving, yet adamant, behavior of individuals needing to be right, felt grating to my spirit.

I found myself "IN the world and OF it." What was I being called to do? Intellectually, I knew the importance of stepping into the awareness of a parallel universe and become the sacred witness...The Watcher, as Jim Rosemergy refers to it! The parallel universe is a dimension right alongside the physical dimension we are currently in. Nearly all factors are the same, except one. In the parallel universe there is total peace and harmony. Was I willing to step out of the unfolding drama and step into the parallel universe right where I was?

At that time, what seemed more important was to take the geographical cure, to leave my home and go to the neighborhood pool just a short distance away. I can do that in January in Florida. I knew I could have distanced myself, energetically, by walking into another room; yet, I felt called to go to the pool where I had gone to pray and send healing energy to individuals in the past.

Exercising in the pool and using my breath to shift my focus away from the horrific images being shown on the TV reminded me what I had been viewing was a reel-life movie! Did I know, at that time, what greater good could be poised to unfold at a later time as a result? No, I didn't consciously know; however, I knew the importance to my spiritual growth to come up higher, to send healing energy to the situation. I, also, knew the importance of giving thanks in advance that ONLY GOOD CAN COME FROM THIS, even though several people returned to spirit (died) as a result! I had no idea how their return to spirit at that time was playing out in each of their life journeys! It was none of my business.

Each one of us is a portal through which a situation can be either escalated or diffused. I chose to see the outcome as exposing that which has been unhealthy and unloving in the attitudes and behaviors of generations of people. It was like a cancer coming to the surface in the consciousness of our country and elsewhere on the planet.

Just as we have decried NEVER AGAIN in so many other situations in our planetary history, and despite the vile nature of the uprising, I chose to hold to the vision of a uniting in consciousness of those who are willing to be part of the solution. It was a critical mass of individuals, working together for peace and justice to be established "on Earth as it is in Heaven."

FROM PEDUNCLE TO THE NEXT PHYLUM

Jesuit priest and paleontologist Pierre Teilhard de Chardin, in his book The Phenomenon of Man, published by Harper Perennial Modern Thought, refers to the experience I described above as a peduncle experience. Teilhard uses the example of a phylum and a peduncle, which might look like an egg-timer or an hour glass. According to Teilhard, humanity evolves, both personally and collectively, through its many growth experiences, like sand flowing upwards in an hourglass.

We live in a phylum, like the bulb on an hourglass. The womb is our earliest example of a phylum It's where our physical lives begin in each chapter of our one ongoing life experience. Using this as an example, the fetus takes its nourishment from its host and grows until the phylum, or womb, can no longer support its growth. Then, at a time known only to that fetus, it begins its exit from the phylum, which is accompanied by contractions. The intensity and duration of the contractions can be different for each birth.

For example, when our first daughter was born, the contractions came fast and furious, and she was born in a little over two hours, from beginning to end. The experience with the birth of our second daughter was the opposite. The contractions began very early each morning for ten days, then stopped by mid-morning. This continued until she was finally ready to make her entrance into our family.

When the fetus is ready to reveal itself as a baby and emerge into its new phylum of the outside world, it must first squeeze through the birth canal, or peduncle. It's like the narrow neck between the two bulbs of the hourglass. A doctor or mid-wife is usually there to coach and support the mother as she's giving birth. Before it's time to push, the coaching is to relax and breathe.

I've given birth four times in this chapter of my ongoing life experience and know the value of this coaching first-hand! At the appropriate time, the caregiver then says PUSH! It isn't beneficial to the birthing process to push before the action is called for. At the appropriate time, the push makes all the difference in facilitating the birth.

Then, at various levels throughout the child's development, the child experiences their own stretching places... learning to walk, talk, tie a shoe lace, use their thinking capacity in school, etc. This supports the child to expand their awareness as a physical, mental, emotional, and spiritual being. Humanity, also, collectively experiences this process!

I believe we on the planet are being poised to enter into a new phylum, and the peduncle experience is part of this process. We have elected to be role-players in this major shift in consciousness unfolding on our planet. If we attempt to delay the process by resisting the birth, the result can be devastating, creating greater complications, just like in the delivery of the new baby! The new Mom is aware of the value of moving through the process, despite all its strong contractions, since she is eager to experience the joy of holding her new baby.

Mom, also, knows that there will be stretching places as the child goes through its own rites of passage, just like in our collective planetary birthing. At each level, a new peduncle experience comes into play, opening the way for the greater experience of opportunities for continued growth, or honing, in preparation for the next new phylum.

I believe what we have been witnessing in our nation and on our planet is the next level of our collective growth process. At each peduncle experience, there may be the outer "weeping and gnashing of teeth," as we read in Matthew 8:12, personally and collectively. We have witnessed it so many times in our nation's history; yet, the inner balance... the silence... is still our saving grace.

The S I L E N C E... I've used this word as an acronym. See if it fits for you ...

Silence

Is

Loving,

Empowering,

Non-resistant,

Compassionate

Energy

As we mindfully step into the parallel universe of the Silence, we are able to engage in our life experiences, yet not be attached to them. Might we still have a preference in the outcome? On a human level, yes; however, we know the importance of healing our human concerns first, surrendering our preferences so that we may show-up as a spiritual support for one another, a mid-wife. The surrender sets-up the sure-end to our concerns. We can be at peace, knowing that we may never fully understand the greater purpose for another's life experiences, or that of our nation. Yet, we may discern glimpses of this greater purpose the more we let go and hold sacred space for the greater purpose to unfold.

We learn to allow experiences to flow in and out of our lives because we know that physical reality is continually changing. This is the highest form of Love we can offer to each other. We are being called to step into a Higher Love that is revolutionary. It's a Love that shakes up the status-quo and prepares the way for the peduncle experience to unfold, with ease and grace. This involves the willingness of each participant. We will move to the next phylum, either by rising into it or by kicking and screaming while being pushed from behind by those on the earth journey with us who are leading the way to the next phylum!

In writing this paragraph I remembered a story I heard many years ago about a monk who lived in a monastery. One day there was a knock at the front door. When he opened the door, a very angry couple handed him a baby, saying their daughter had accused him of being the baby's father, and it was his responsibility to raise the little boy. The monk knew he hadn't fathered the child, yet he took the baby with a simple "Ah, so" and, without any defense on his part, lovingly raised him like his own child.

Some years later, after the boy had matured to a young man, the monk answered another knock at the door. It was the same parents, saying their daughter had wrongly accused him, and they were there to reclaim their grandchild. The monk non-resistantly released the young man to his grandparents with a simple "Ah, so..." and returned to his daily activities at the monastery.

One might marvel at the patience and practice it must have taken for the monk to show-up with that attitude. Yet, was it about attitude or was it simply who he was as an individual. Showing-up in any other way would not have been in-line with his true nature as a spiritual being. The child was raised in a loving atmosphere that nurtured his development on all levels...physically, mentally, emotionally, and spiritually. He was given tools with which to navigate his future life experiences, as well as to be an example to his birth family.

Many of us may not have been nurtured in a healthy environment as a child. Yet, as we become willing to re-parent ourselves and treat ourselves with love and respect, we create a healthier place within, which translates to a healthier life experience. There is the utmost value in letting go of any need to blame and hold others responsible for what may be perceived as lack in our lives.

As we do, it sends a message to the universe that we are now ready to receive the greater good which has always been ours from the beginning. Even brief moments of stillness, retreating from the world of form, and breathing in "ah"... then exhaling "so" ...can release angst, stress, concern, or any other unhealthy energy that keeps us in our separate mind.

The S T I L L N E S S... that place within that is anchored in the awareness of our Oneness with all Life. This is the gift that keeps on giving and continually maintains a place of B A L A N C E within. We experience the flexibility of shifting our mental and emotional stance while being grounded in the awareness that no one and no thing is against us. We become like the Tai Chi Master who can, in an instant, gently move his or her body to avert or avoid any outer attack without moving away from the center of balance.

The master prepares him or herself with daily practice to hone this flexibility. We come to the place where we have prepared ourselves to serve as the sacred witness,   not by filling ourselves with words. On the contrary, it's by emptying ourselves. We are no longer weighted-down by the emotional baggage of the human self. This practice enables us to gently RISE above any outer turmoil and SHINE our inner Light which is no longer obstructed by the presence of *squigglies.*

Questions to ponder...

1. As you glean a new awareness of yourself as a spiritual being learning through this human experience, how has your understanding of your past choices changed?

2. On a scale of 1-10, 10 being the highest level of comfort, how comfortable are you identifying the spiritual aspect of you as "The Christ?"

3. If your answer to #2 was less than a #6, what would it take to raise it to a #7 or higher?

CHAPTER ELEVEN

Practices For Anchoring
Our Spiritual Nature

*"May I live this day compassionate of heart,
clear in word, gracious in awareness, courageous in thought,
generous in love."*—John O'Donahue

I'd like to share with you the following Prayer of the Chalice (original author unknown) which has been part of my daily spiritual practice for more than 30 years, morning and night. Actually, I set my alarm to wake up ten minutes before I want to get out of bed. When the alarm buzzes, I push snooze so I may utilize the nine minutes to focus my mind and heart on anchoring myself in a place of balance for my day, using this prayer and not falling back to sleep. (The number 9 in Numerology represents change.) Later that morning I use it again, by aligning it with the first part of the Tai Chi form which is a daily practice.

There are often times during the day when I simply bring to mind the first line of the prayer, "Today I raise my whole being, a vessel emptied of self." This practice instantly brings me back to my center, as I breathe in and feel my energy being lifted, then empty the breath and feel anchored again in the Stillness within. It is what A Course in Miracles calls the "Holy Instant."

As I lay my head on the pillow at bedtime, I allow my breath and the energy from the prayer to clear my human energy on all levels so I may drift off to a restful sleep. This prepares me to awaken the next morning with clarity and vitality! The prayer can, also, be aligned with the Sun Salutation in Yoga, for those of you who may use this practice. I share it with you in the form to which I have revised it, which fits my present understanding...

The Prayer of the Chalice
as Affirmative Prayer

(revised by Ann Marie Acacio)

Today I raise my whole being,
a vessel emptied of self. I offer
this my emptiness and am so filled
with Divine Light, and Love, and Life,
that these precious gifts radiate
through me and overflow the
chalice of my heart into the
hearts of all with whom I
come in contact this day,
revealing to them
the beauty of
Divine Joy
and
Wholeness
and
the
Serenity
and Peace
which nothing can destroy.

Each week I receive a group email from my friend, Rev. Jim Calderone, which I find meaningful, and I especially enjoy his original poetry. One week Jim shared an idea that touched the very core of my being, and I'm grateful for his permission to share it with you...

"More and more I have come to realize that there must have been something about Jesus' very presence which transformed the space around him in such a way that all who stepped into that space found themselves in a place where life could begin again, right there!"

We can, also, substitute The Buddha, Krishna, Mohammed, or the name of any other spiritual master that is meaningful to us in this statement.

At each opportunity I ask myself "what am I willing to communicate by my very presence in this situation?" It's NOT about the other person! It's about how I, how WE, choose to BE the Presence, living, moving, and having Its very Being in and through us.

Most importantly, living in our rightful place is the commitment to live in gratitude...giving thanks in advance, for the blessed opportunity to show-up as a bringer of the Light, a conduit. We consciously allow the Light from the super-conscious area of our One Mind to radiate through our centered and focused awareness.

Our very presence becomes a beacon which transforms the space around us and welcomes others into this space where they may also find their own Light for their Journey.

In closing, I offer the following Franciscan Benediction, which I have revised as an Affirmative Prayer. It has called me for many years to Rise and Shine, which is actually what my Dad used to say to me whenever he awakened me in the morning! May it serve as a nudge to awaken you to Rise and Shine right where you're planted.

A Franciscan Benediction

May you be blessed with discomfort at easy answers, half truths, and superficial relationships, so that you may live deep within your heart.

May you be blessed with anger at injustice, oppression, and exploitation of people, so that you may work for justice, freedom and peace.

May you be blessed with tears to shed for those who suffer from pain, rejection, starvation, and war, so that you may reach out your hand to comfort them and to turn their pain into joy.

And may you be blessed with enough foolishness to believe that you can make a difference in this world, so that you can do what others claim cannot be done.

My goal as a teacher and minister is to move you out of your comfort zone so that you may take up residence in the abode of peace and balance that has always been within you. Blessings to you, my friend, as you reclaim your rightful place... in the Trinity,,, in the Omniverse, right within you. LIVE from this ascended knowingness AS your capital "T" Truth! **"Ah, so!"**

Namaste'...

I honor the place in You where the Universe resides.
I honor the place in You where lies your love and your light,

And your truth and your uniqueness.
I honor the place in you where if you are in that place in You,

And I am in that place in me, there is only One of us.

"And those who were seen dancing were thought to be insane by those who could not hear the music."

—Nietzsche

Acknowledgements

My special thanks are extended to the following people who have partnered with me to bring this book to fruition...

- the students in the Lessons in Truth class many years ago who were present and created the field of consciousness which set the stage for the material to be birthed through me. I am eternally grateful!

- Rev. Linda Martella-Whitsett and Rev. Jim Rosemergy for their loving support in reviewing the manuscript and gifting me with their heart-felt endorsements.

- My very creative and intuitive granddaughter Samantha Lynn Acacio who masterfully and lovingly created all the diagrams for this book.

- Tom Harrington, a long-time friend and former student, whose creative skills as a graphic artist brought to life the vision I held for the cover of this book.

- Diane Dean, a wonderful friend who is part of a Writers' Critique Group and blessed me with her expertise and invaluable critique, with LOTS of red ink on the pages!

- Ellen Raineri, a great friend and former student, who shared valuable input at the book's completion in reviewing it with a metaphysical understanding.

All my students and workshop participants who served as a sounding board each time I presented the ideas and encouraged me to put them in writing for posterity.

I am extremely grateful to have been used as a vehicle for this material to be made known in the realm of form. Each presentation of the material continues to bring an added measure of enrichment to my soul. It is my Gift to share it with you.

If you have questions about the material or would like to share an insight, please feel free to contact me...

Ann Marie Acacio

youriseandshine@outlook.com

About the Author

Born and raised in Wilkes-Barre, PA, Rev. Ann Marie Acacio, with the support of her husband Bob and other interested Unity friends, began the first Unity ministry in NE Pennsylvania in September 1979. She felt blessed to celebrate the ministry's 40th anniversary with them in 2019.

Ann Marie graduated from the Advanced Training program in Unity School of Christianity in 1983 and was licensed as a teacher of metaphysical studies by Unity Worldwide Ministries in 1984. She continued to serve as Spiritual Leader and was accepted into the then-newly-created Field Licensing and Ordination Program at Unity in 1992, culminating in Ordination in May 1996.

She served on the Board of Unity Worldwide Ministries, Eastern Region for 10 years, including four years as president before her retirement in 2006. She served on Community of Inter-Faith Action (CIFA) and was a member of the Wyoming Valley Interfaith Council for 18 years, acting as president for six years.

Ann Marie has served in prison ministry for over 30 years and as Chaplain, conducting Chapel Services at various nursing and retirement homes. After retirement as senior minister of Unity Church in Wilkes-Barre, she started a wedding ministry in NE Pennsylvania, which she has now re-established in central Florida, since moving to The Villages.

She is also a certified Life Coach and Group Coach, having graduated from the Academy for Coaching Excellence in 2005.

Rev. Ann Marie and her husband, Bob, will celebrate 58 years of marriage in August 2021 with their 3 adult children and their spouses, nine grandchildren and six great-grandchildren. Her passion is (as she puts it) "being an itinerant teacher like my good Jewish friend Jesus!"

She considers herself most blessed and very grateful!